21st
Century
Skills Library

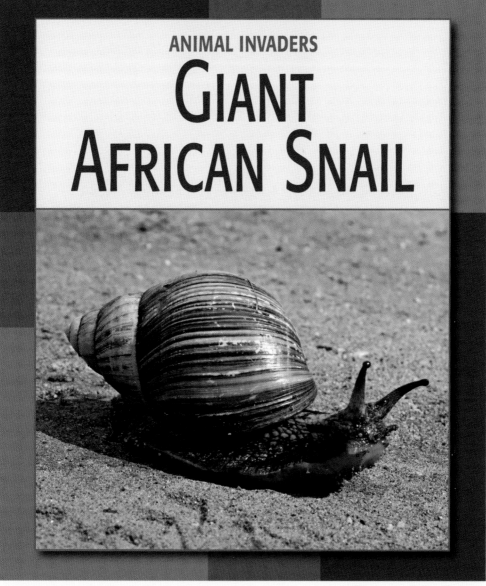

ANIMAL INVADERS

GIANT
AFRICAN SNAIL

Susan H. Gray

Cherry Lake Publishing
Ann Arbor, Michigan

CHERRY
LAKE
Publishing

Published in the United States of America by Cherry Lake Publishing
Ann Arbor, MI
www.cherrylakepublishing.com

Content Adviser: J. James Murray Jr., PhD, Professor of Biology Emeritus, University of
Virginia, Charlottesville, Virginia

Please note: Our map is as up-to-date as possible at the time of publication.

Photo Credits: Cover and pages 1 and 4, ©Danita Delimont/Alamy; page 6,
©HoltStudios International/Alamy; pages 9 and 22, ©Renee Morris/Alamy; page 11,
©FLPA/Alamy; page 12, ©istockphoto.com/Kevin Lindeque; page 14, ©Stephen
Shepherd/Alamy; page 16, ©Jeannette Lambert, used under license from Shutterstock,
Inc.; page 19, ©nicholasbird/Alamy; page 20, ©David G. Robinson, USDA APHIS PPQ,
Bugwood.org; page 24, ©perfectpicture/alamy

Map by XNR Productions Inc.

Library of Congress Cataloging-in-Publication Data
Gray, Susan Heinrichs.
 Giant African snail / by Susan H. Gray.
   p. cm.—(Animal invaders)
 Includes index.
 ISBN-13: 978-1-60279-241-8
 ISBN-10: 1-60279-241-0
 1. Giant African snail—Juvenile literature. I. Title. II. Series.
 QL430.5.A22G73 2009
 594'.38—dc22   2008000803

*Cherry Lake Publishing would like to acknowledge the work of
The Partnership for 21st Century Skills.
Please visit www.21stcenturyskills.org for more information.*

TABLE OF CONTENTS

CHAPTER ONE

DINING FROM DUSK UNTIL DAWN

A giant African snail searches for its next meal.

The sun is setting and the large snails are beginning to move about the garden. One snail glides forward over the smooth surface of a tomato. As the snail moves, it eats nonstop.

The snail's mouth is an opening on the underside of the animal's body. This opening presses firmly against the tomato skin. Each time the mouth opens, a rough, tonguelike strap rakes across the tomato. The strap sweeps shreds of tomato flesh into the snail's mouth.

The snail keeps this up all night. Not far away, other snails are rapidly consuming broccoli, melons, and cucumbers. As they glide along eating, they leave a trail of damaged rinds, chewed-up stalks, and slimy leaves. By morning, most vegetables in this garden will bear the scars of the snails' visit.

21st Century Content

Giant African snails are an invasive **species**. A species is a group of similar plants or animals. Human beings, gray wolves, and giant African snails are all different species. If something is invasive, it has moved in and taken over. Human activity usually introduces invasive species to new areas.

A global organization called the Invasive Species Specialist Group (ISSG) works to raise awareness of the problems that such invaders cause. The ISSG is made up of more than 140 experts from all over the world. They have created a list of almost 500 invasive plants and animals as well as a list of the world's 100 worst invaders. The giant African snail is on this worst-invader list.

A snail's body produces a thick, slimy fluid called **mucus**. This helps the animal glide over a surface. Large snails such as the giant African snail create a wide trail of slime. The slime may contain disease-causing germs. Therefore, people who handle the snails should always wash their hands afterward. Keeping hands clean is an important step to take in order to avoid getting sick and spreading germs to others.

These animals are giant African snails, or *Achatina fulica*. They eat almost any fruit or vegetable they find. And that's not all they do.

This adult giant African snail eats its way through a piece of lettuce.

CHAPTER TWO

THE TALE OF A SNAIL

The giant African snail is the largest land snail on Earth. An adult can weigh as much as 2 pounds (about 1 kilogram)!

The animal lives in a pointed, spiral shell. Giant African snail shells are usually brown or reddish brown with yellow streaks. Adult shells have as many as nine **whorls**, or complete turns in their spiral. Shells may reach lengths of 8 inches (20 centimeters). That's about as long as a new pencil. However, most giant African snails are less than half that length.

Snails are members of a large group of animals called **gastropods**. The word *gastropod* means "stomach-foot." It refers to the fact that the animal has one large foot on the stomach side of its body. Actually, the snail's stomach is located up inside the shell, with most of its other organs. Slugs are also gastropods.

The foot is the body part that you can see most easily. At the foot's front end is the snail's head, with a mouth and two pairs of feelers. The feelers are used for touching, smelling, and seeing.

Snails eat by using a long mouthpart called the **radula**. It is covered by hundreds of tiny teeth. As the snail moves along, it opens its mouth and sweeps the radula across the food. The radula scrapes tiny bits of food into the snail's mouth.

Giant African snails are **nocturnal**. That means they are most active at night. They come out to feed on all sorts of plants after sunset. In fact, they eat more than 500 different kinds of plants. They feed on living plants as well as dead, rotting ones.

Like most snails, the giant African snail has two sets of feelers on its head. The snail uses them to smell, see, and touch its surroundings.

Young snails dine on only a few types of plant. As they get older, they feed on a wider variety of plants. The adults eat beans, peas, carrots, onions, and rice. They also eat

pumpkins, potatoes, and papayas. It's not just crops they go for. The snails also eat flowers and decorative garden plants.

Giant African snails start life as tiny eggs. The eggs may take several weeks to hatch. The temperature and dampness must be just right.

When the tiny snails finally hatch, the first thing they do is eat their own eggshells! They sometimes eat the shells of the unhatched snails, too. This provides calcium, a material they need to grow their new spiral shells.

Young snails develop quickly. They become adults at about six months of age and begin laying their own eggs. Giant African snails usually lay between 100

3 1833 05508 8436

Giant African snails lay their eggs in clusters.

and 500 eggs at a time. They lay them in clusters, often just beneath the soil surface.

If they survive to adulthood, the snails usually live to be about five years of age. But snails as old as nine have been reported.

Giant African snails stop moving and eating to save their energy during the warm, dry season. They also pull their bodies into their shells. Can you guess what season this giant African snail is in?

Giant African snails live in many kinds of **habitats**. They do well in warm, humid areas, where there is plenty of food. They live on farmland, wetlands, and riverbanks as well as in gardens and forests.

During the very dry, warm time of year, usually in summer, the giant African snail **estivates**, or slows down its body functions. The snail pulls into its shell. Its breathing and heart rates fall. It stops eating and crawling, saving energy for the next season, when water is plentiful.

At one time, giant African snails lived only in eastern Africa. They now live in western Africa, Brazil, China, and India. They also live on many of the world's tropical and subtropical islands.

Learning & Innovation Skills

Different animals have different ways of slowing down their body functions during challenging conditions. Animals that **hibernate**, such as dormice or bats, shut down in the cold of winter. Animals that estivate, such as the giant African snail, shut down during the dry periods of summer. When animals hibernate or estivate, their breathing and heart rates slow down. They eat little or nothing and use very little energy. Before an animal enters this state, it finds a place where it is safe from its enemies. Why would it do this?

CHAPTER THREE

OUT OF AFRICA

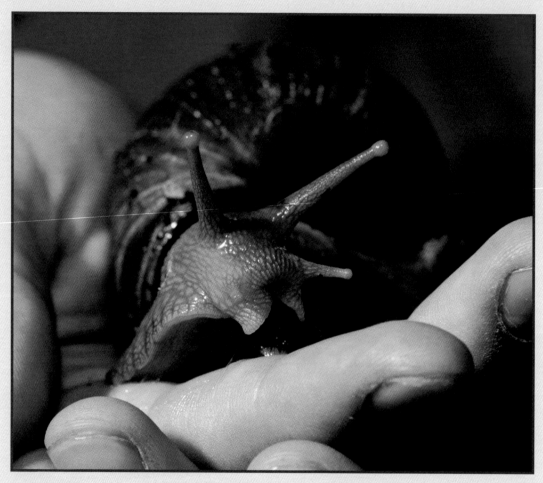

Giant African snails live where they don't belong because of human activity.

Giant African snails have moved into other countries in many ways. They have traveled on cargo ships. They have been brought to new countries as a food supply. And they have been hidden secretly inside luggage. No matter how they came, giant African snails have created problems in every country they have invaded.

Most giant African snails have traveled by ship to new countries. Cargo ships visit ports all over the world, carrying crates of food, clothing, and many other items. Quite often, they are carrying giant African snails as well. Adult snails might be hiding in bunches of bananas. Young snails might be creeping among boxes of mangoes. Snail eggs might be stuck to flower bulbs.

In Brazil, people brought in the snails on purpose—to eat! Diners around the world love **escargot**, an expensive snail cooked with special sauces. Some people thought that giant African snails would make a better choice for escargot. These snails are large, grow quickly, and can be healthier than the usual escargot snails. So people brought in the snails and started farms.

A seafood market in Paris, France, sells stuffed escargot snails. Traditional escargot snails are much smaller than giant African snails.

But there was a problem. Giant African snails are as tough as boots and difficult to chew!

With no reason to keep the snails, farmers released the animals into their gardens and yards. It did not take long for the snails to multiply and spread. Experts now fear that they will spread to other South American countries.

Giant African snails have entered the United States many times. People have stopped them everywhere but in Hawaii. After World War II (1939–1945), U.S. soldiers were returning from other countries with their equipment. Some of that equipment carried giant African snails. Luckily, inspectors at U.S. ports stopped the snails dozens of times.

Sometimes, the snails travel in people's luggage. In 1966, a boy from Florida secretly brought three snails home after a trip to Hawaii. The boy's grandmother later put the snails in her garden. Right away, they began laying eggs and multiplying. By 1973, about 18,000 giant African snails were living in Florida.

21st Century Content

People who visit other countries often bring back special items and gifts. They cannot bring back whatever they want, however. For example, it is against the law to bring in some plants and animals that might carry diseases. It is also illegal to bring in certain invasive plant and animal species. Citizens traveling to foreign countries need to be informed about laws that might affect them.

In 1958, a young boy was traveling through Arizona with his family after a trip to Hawaii. He had hidden in his suitcase some giant African snails that he had found in Hawaii. When the family stopped to visit a wild animal farm, the boy left his snails with the owner. Soon afterward, the owner advertised that he had giant African snails. When government workers saw the ad, they hurried to the farm. They told the owner that the snails caused serious problems and must be destroyed. How could this kind of situation have been avoided?

Government workers and snail experts spent 10 years getting rid of the invaders.

In 2004, government workers again found giant African snails in the United States. This time, pet store owners and schoolteachers were at fault. In nine states, pet store owners were selling the snails to animal lovers, and teachers were using them in their classrooms. Fortunately, government workers were able to round up all those snails, and none of the animals had spread into the wild.

CHAPTER FOUR

WHAT'S THE PROBLEM?

Giant African snails are hardy animals that can survive in many different habitats.

Snails of all kinds live in all sorts of places in many different countries. They live on land, in salty ocean waters, and in freshwater lakes and streams. They eat plants, decaying matter, and sometimes even other snails. So what is the problem with giant African snails?

This large group of giant African snails climbs a tree on the Caribbean island of Saint Lucia.

Giant African snails create many different problems. They destroy gardens and crops. They can carry diseases. They foul the air and roadways. These snails can cause serious problems for the local plants and animals.

Giant African snails upset the **ecosystem** in several ways. These large snails eat much of the food that would go to smaller snails and other animals. When they die, their large shells crumble into the ground, adding calcium to the soil. That changes the kinds of plants that can grow in the soil.

On some Japanese islands, the snails have made one problem even worse. An invasive species of toad has lived on the islands for years. It eats different animals, and it produces a poison that kills attackers. When the giant African snail was brought to these islands, the toad gained a new food source. It could eat the giant snails. Now, one invasive species is helping another invasive species survive!

The snails cause great harm to crops. They damage or destroy fields of potatoes, yams, beans, and peanuts. They move up trees and along limbs, eating coconut leaves, bananas, and many other food plants. In India, the giant African snail eats its way through rice paddies.

The injury to crops is far-reaching. For example, a giant African snail eats only some of the rind of a melon. But then no one will ship it or buy it. Farmers cannot even feed the damaged food to their livestock for fear of making the animals sick.

A giant African snail produces a trail of mucus. The mucus can carry disease as well as create a slimy mess.

Gardeners also have problems with giant African snails. The snails eat expensive flowers and decorative plants. It does not take long for the huge snails to destroy an entire garden.

Giant African snails can also carry **organisms** that cause serious problems. A type of worm that lives in the snail's body causes a brain disease in humans. People who eat raw or undercooked snails are at risk of getting this dangerous disease. They come down with headaches, tingling in the skin, muscle aches, and high fever.

Where snails are present in high numbers, they create yet another problem—foul and dangerous sidewalks and roads. Their rotting bodies leave a terrible odor as well as a slimy mess. That mess can cause vehicles to skid out of control.

Some people like to keep giant African snails as pets. The snails eat almost anything. They don't need much more than an empty glass tank, a filled water dish, and some leaves to eat. Snails kept in tanks seem fairly harmless. So why do you think it is against the law in the United States to keep them as pets?

CHAPTER FIVE

How to Derail This Snail

*A young person holds a giant African snail
at a museum demonstration.*

Scientists have tried different ways of controlling giant African snails or removing them from areas where they don't belong. In some countries, their plans have worked. In other countries, their plans have failed—or made matters worse.

In the United States, the snails have appeared in several states. They were discovered in most cases before they became a problem. Inspectors in California have spotted them dozens of times and nabbed them before they could spread.

But Florida and Hawaii were not so fortunate. The Florida population started most likely with the trio of snails in the grandmother's garden. From there, it grew to thousands. So government workers and snail experts laid out a plan. They used poisoned bait to attract and kill the snails. They also collected snails by hand. It took about 10 years and about $1 million to wipe out the Florida snails completely.

In Hawaii, things have turned out much worse. Giant African snails have lived on this string of U.S. islands in the Pacific Ocean since the 1930s. Homeowners brought them in to decorate their gardens. But then the snails

began to spread. They threatened crops, farms, and orchards.

Finally, the U.S. government set up **quarantines**. Laws kept people from moving the snails between islands. It became illegal for people to own the snails. Officials also brought in animal species that eat giant African snails. Fourteen of those species were actually snail-eating snails. Despite all these efforts, the giant African snail has continued to spread. And one of those snail-eating snails has become a pest in its own right!

On some Pacific islands, people have used poison bait to kill the snails. Some bait kills snails that simply crawl over it.

Other bait must be eaten. However, people must use any poison with great care. Poison can kill other animal species. It can also harm farm animals and pets.

It is clear that the best way to control giant African snails is to keep them from invading in the first place. Many countries now have laws to prevent invasions. Laws require airport workers to carefully inspect travelers' bags. Ship inspectors search cargo very closely. Pet store owners are not allowed to sell the snails. Unless everyone remains watchful, these creeping invaders will damage crops and threaten human health in even greater numbers.

Farming officials in the United States are constantly keeping an eye out for the giant African snail. They are also watching out for the giant Ghana tiger snail and the banana rasp snail. These two snails are closely related to the giant African snail, and they can also destroy crops. Neither snail is listed as an invasive species in the United States, but it is important to be prepared.

The success of any invasive species action program depends on different groups working together. That includes federal, state, and local officials, university researchers, public health agencies, and state and local law officials as well as the public.

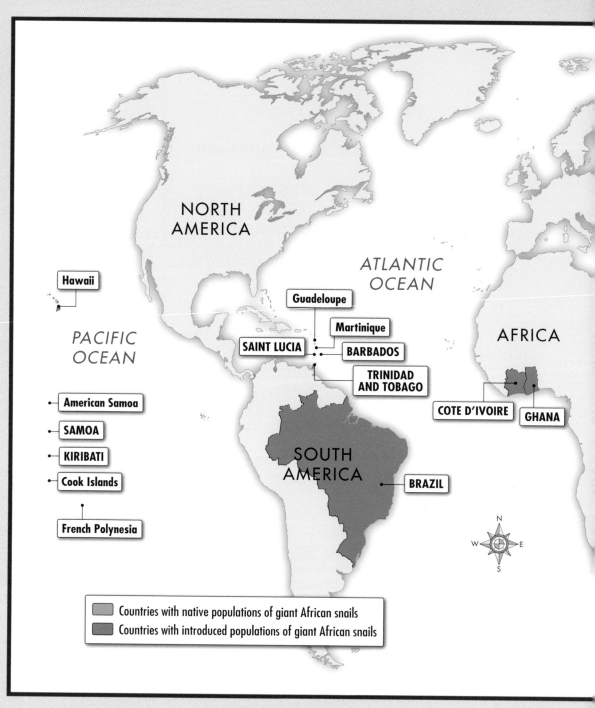

Countries with native populations of giant African snails
Countries with introduced populations of giant African snails

This map shows where in the world the giant African snail

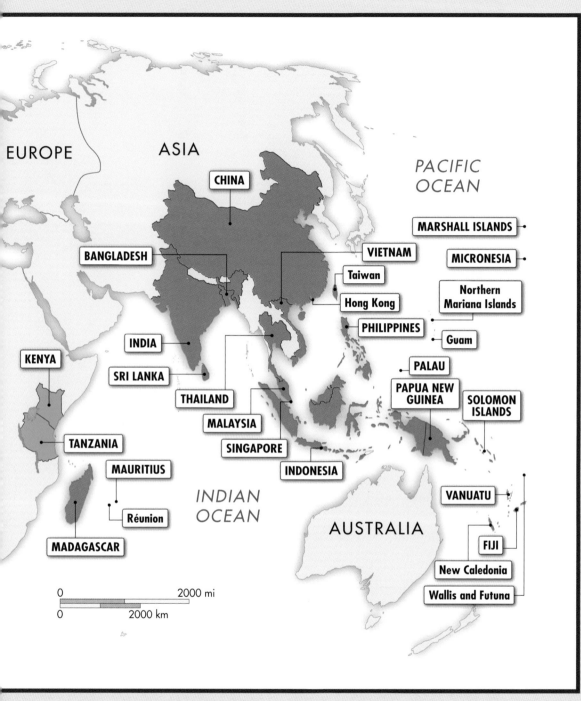

EUROPE

ASIA

PACIFIC
OCEAN

CHINA

MARSHALL ISLANDS

MICRONESIA

BANGLADESH

VIETNAM

Taiwan

Northern
Mariana Islands

Hong Kong

PHILIPPINES

Guam

INDIA

KENYA

SRI LANKA

PALAU

PAPUA NEW
GUINEA

SOLOMON
ISLANDS

THAILAND

TANZANIA

MALAYSIA

MAURITIUS

SINGAPORE

INDONESIA

Réunion

INDIAN
OCEAN

VANUATU

AUSTRALIA

MADAGASCAR

FIJI

New Caledonia

0   2000 mi

0   2000 km

Wallis and Futuna

lives naturally and where it has invaded.

GLOSSARY

ecosystem (EE-koh-siss-tuhm) a community of plants, animals, and other organisms together with their environment, working as a unit

escargot (ess-kar-GO) a snail prepared for people to eat

estivate (ESS-tiv-AYT) to spend the summer in an inactive state, with slow heart and breathing rates

gastropods (GASS-truh-podz) mollusks that have a head with feelers, a fleshy foot that helps the animal move, and often a spiral shell; snails and slugs are gastropods

habitats (HAB-ih-tats) the areas where plants or animals normally live

hibernate (HYE-bur-nate) to spend the winter in an inactive state, with slow heart and breathing rates

mollusks (MOL-uhsks) animals with soft bodies, no backbone, and usually a hard outer shell; snails, clams, and octopuses are mollusks

mucus (MYOO-kuhss) a thick, slimy fluid released by the skin of snails and slugs to help them glide over surfaces

nocturnal (nok-TUR-nuhl) active at night

organisms (OR-guh-niz-uhmz) individual forms of life, such as plants, animals, or bacteria

quarantines (KWAR-uhn-teenz) periods during which no movement of people or objects is permitted in order to stop the spread of a problem or disease

radula (RAD-yoo-luh) a long mouthpart covered by hundreds of tiny teeth that help a gastropod tear its food

species (SPEE-sheez) a group of similar plants or animals

whorls (HWOR-ulz) complete turns of a spiral shell

FOR MORE INFORMATION

Books

DK Publishing. *E.encyclopedia Animal*. New York: DK Children, 2005.

Gilpin, Daniel. *Snails, Shellfish & Other Mollusks*.
Minneapolis: Compass Point Books, 2006.

Legg, Gerald. *Minibeasts*. North Mankato, MN: Chrysalis Education, 2003.

Web Sites

Exotic Plant Pests—Giant African Snail
www2.dpi.qld.gov.au/health/5613.html
To learn more about the giant African snail and how it once invaded Australia

Global Invasive Species Database: *Achatina fulica*
www.issg.org/database/species/ecology.asp?si=64&fr=1&sts=sss
To find out more about this invading snail

Not All Alien Invaders Are from Outer Space
www.aphis.usda.gov/lpa/pubs/invasive/16asnail.html
To read about the giant African snail on a related U.S. Department of Agriculture site

INDEX

ABOUT THE AUTHOR

Susan H. Gray has a master's degree in zoology. She has written more than 90 science and reference books for children, and especially loves writing about animals. Gray also likes to garden and play the piano. She lives in Cabot, Arkansas, with her husband, Michael, and many pets.